Workbook

WORLD ENGLISH 3

Real People • Real Places • Real Language

Kristin L. Johannsen

T0343871

HEINLE
CENGAGE Learning™

Australia • Brazil • Japan • Korea • Mexico • Singapore • Spain • United Kingdom • United States

HEINLE
CENGAGE Learning™

World English 3 Workbook
Real People • Real Places • Real Language
Kristin L. Johannsen

Publisher: Jason Mann

Commissioning Editor: Carol Goodwright

Development Editor: Louisa Essenhigh

Technology Development Manager: Debie Mirtle

Director of Global Marketing: Ian Martin

Product Manager: Ruth McAleavey

Content Project Editor: Amy Smith

ELT Production Controller: Denise Power

Cover Designer: Page 2 LLC

Compositor: MPS Limited, A Macmillan Company

Head of Production and Manufacturing: Alissa Chappell

ISBN: 978-1-111-21770-9

Heinle, Cengage Learning
Cheriton House
North Way
Andover
Hampshire
SP10 5BE
United Kingdom

Cengage Learning is a leading provider of customized learning solutions with office locations around the globe, including Singapore, the United Kingdom, Australia, Mexico, Brazil, and Japan. Locate your local office at: **international.cengage.com/region**

Cengage Learning products are represented in Canada by Nelson Education, Ltd.

Visit Heinle online at **elt.heinle.com**

Visit our corporate website at **www.cengage.com**

Cover photo: Stephen Alvarez/National Geographic Image Collection, Wadi Dirbat, Sultanate of Oman

Printed in China
3 4 5 6 7 8 9 10 – 15 14 13 12 11

CONTENTS

SCOPE AND SEQUENCE

	Grammar	Vocabulary	Communication	Reading and Writing
People and Places page 7				
UNIT 1	Present perfect continuous tense *So* + adjective + *that*	Migration Climate	Giving reasons for living in a particular place and for moving to another place	"Australia, the International Nation" Giving reasons for migration
The Mind page 13				
UNIT 2	Gerunds as subjects and after prepositions *May, might* and *could* for possibility	Thought processes Scientific investigations	Describing physical sensations Describing fears and being nervous	"The Mind-Body Connection" Giving an opinion about the effect of mind over body
Changing Planet page 19				
UNIT 3	Passive voice: all tenses Past perfect tense	Environmental changes Large numbers	Offering suggestions to save energy at school Linking words	"What Can One City Do?" Offering suggestions to save energy
Money page 25				
UNIT 4	Gerund vs. infinitive Review of the passive voice	Money transactions Banking	Explaining the value of prized possessions	"Banknotes: Facts about Paper Money" Describing national currency
Survival page 31				
UNIT 5	Unreal conditional *Wish*	Survival skills Environmental conservation	Simulating emergency situations	"Ready for Anything" Plans for an emergency situation
Art page 37				
UNIT 6	Reported speech Subject adjective clauses	Art Art materials	Describing art, suggesting titles, and exhibit areas	"Biographies of Great Artists: Frida Kahlo" Describing a painting

	Grammar	Vocabulary	Communication	Reading and Writing
Transportation page 43				
UNIT 7	Passive voice: present continuous tense and present perfect tense Indirect questions	Methods of communication Sensory adjectives	Using polite questions	"Streets for People" Describing walking in your city
Competition page 49				
UNIT 8	Negative questions Object adjective clauses	Sportsmanship Sports	Choosing a sport to match a person's personality	"Voice Your Opinion: *Change Is Needed in Youth Sports*" Giving an opinion about competition in children's sports
Danger page 55				
UNIT 9	Tag questions Adverbial clauses of time	Dangerous things Expressions for emergencies	Choosing someone for a dangerous job	"Your Turn: Should Risky Sports Be Banned?" Giving an opinion about risky sports
Mysteries page 61				
UNIT 10	Modals for speculating about the past Future in the past	Investigating mysteries Reactions to surprise	Choosing a mystery you would like to solve	"The Mysteries of Nazca" Giving an opinion about the importance of solving mysteries
Learning page 67				
UNIT 11	*Should have, would have, could have* Noun clauses	Education University majors	Matching learning styles to specific activities	"Students Return from Adventure Abroad" Describing a lesson learned from a difficult experience
Space page 73				
UNIT 12	Future tenses Future modals	Space exploration Future time expressions	Selecting a "citizen astronaut"	"First in Space" Giving an opinion about government spending on space exploration

ILLUSTRATION

9, 10: National Geographic Maps; **23:** Patrick Gnan/IllustrationOnline.com; **27:** Ted Hammond/IllustrationOnline.com; **31:** (l) Ted Hammond/IllustrationOnline.com, (all others) Ralph Voltz/IllustrationOnline.com; **33:** Ralph Voltz/IllustrationOnline.com; **35, 39:** Patrick Gnan/IllustrationOnline.com; **44, 51:** Nesbitt Graphics, Inc.; **62:** (t) National Geographic Maps; **63:** (all) Keith Neely/IllustrationOnline.com; **71:** National Geographic Maps.

PHOTO

7: (t) Constance McGuire/iStockphoto, (b) Heiko Bennewitz/iStockphoto; **8:** (t) Marty Heitner/iStockphoto, (m) Lester Waller/iStockphoto, (b) Michael Krinke/iStockphoto; **10:** Photononstop/SuperStock; **11:** Cannon Collection/Australian Picture Library/Corbis; **12:** Alaska Stock Images/National Geographic Image Collection; **13:** (t) Juan Velasco/National Geographic Image Collection, (b) BananaStock/JupiterImages; **14:** Suprijono Suharjoto/Dreamstime, Tõnis Valing/Dreamstime; **15:** (t) Fotosin/Shutterstock, (b) Tepikina Nastya/Shutterstock; **16:** (background) Monkeybusinessimages/Dreamstime, (t) Joseph Jean Rolland Dubé/iStockphoto, (m) PhotostoGo.com, (b) Steve Cole/iStockphoto; **17:** Ray Fisher/Time Life Pictures/Getty Images; **18:** Sebastian Kaulitzki/iStockphoto; **19:** (t) Amber Antozak/iStockphoto, (b) Irochka Tischenko/iStockphoto; **20:** (l to r) Thomas J. Abercrombie/National Geographic Image Collection, Yellowj/Shutterstock, photos.com, Chieh Cheng/iStockphoto, iStockphoto; **21:** (t to b) Robert Churchill/iStockphoto, Wayne Stadler/iStockphoto, Kevin Russ/iStockphoto, Thomas Perkins/iStockphoto; **22:** (t) Christina Richards/iStockphoto, (m) iStockphoto, (b) Cameron Whitman/iStockphoto; **24:** Jordan Tan/Shutterstock; **25:** (t) Sebastian Czapnik/Dreamstime, (b) Zhang Bo/iStockphoto; **26:** (t) Melissa Carroll/iStockphoto, (m) iStockphoto, (b) Murat Boylu/iStockphoto; **27:** (t) Jeffrey Smith/iStockphoto, (b) Christine Kublanski/iStockphoto; **28:** (t) photos.com, (b) David Ward/iStockphoto; **29:** (t) Neale Cousland/Shutterstock, (b) YellowCrest Media/Shutterstock; **30:** Christophe Testi/Shutterstock; **31:** (tl) Konstantin Mironov/Shutterstock, (tr) Rui Pestana/iStockphoto, (m) Rapid Eye Media/iStockphoto, (b) Joseph Nickischer/iStockphoto; **32:** (t) Sophia Tsibikaki/iStockphoto, (b) Özgür Donmaz/iStockphoto; **34:** (t) Bruce Dale/National Geographic Image Collection, (m) Michael Nichols/National Geographic Image Collection, (b) Lisa F. Young/iStockphoto; **36:** Monkey Business Images/Shutterstock; **37:** (t) iStockphoto (b) Mark Yuill/iStockphoto; **38:** (1) Liliya Kulianionak/Dreamstime, (2) photos.com (3), Konstantins Visnevskis/Shutterstock, (4) Lenny712/Dreamstime; **40:** (t both) The Art Archive/Dolores Olmedo Mexico/Gianni Dagli Orti. © 2009 Banco de México Diego Rivera & Frida Kahlo Museums Trust, Mexico, D. F./Artists Rights Society (ARS), (b) The Art Archive/Museum of Modern Art Mexico/Gianni Dagli Orti. © 2009 Banco de México Diego Rivera & Frida Kahlo Museums Trust, Mexico, D. F./Artists Rights Society (ARS); **41:** Alfonso Rangel/Dreamstime; **42:** Willie B. Thomas/iStockphoto; **43:** (t to b) Tim Jenner/Shutterstock, Ramon Berk/Shutterstock, Jose Gil/Shutterstock, Andres Balcazar/iStockphoto, photos.com; **44:** (t to b) photos.com, René Mansi/iStockphoto, bubamarac/Shutterstock, Paul Prescott/Shutterstock; **45:** (t to b) Eliza Snow/iStockphoto, Stephen Coburn/Shutterstock, iStockphoto, Eyespeak/Shutterstock, Asier Villafranca/Shutterstock; **46:** Jose AS Reyes/Shutterstock; **47:** (t) photos.com, (m) Simon Krzic/Dreamstime, (b) iStockphoto; **48:** egd/Shutterstock; **49:** (t) Elena Weber/Dreamstime, (bl) Jacom Stephens/iStockphoto, (br) iStockphoto; **50:** (l) Stephanie Swartz/iStockphoto, (r) iStockphoto; **51:** (t) Jim Kolaczko/iStockphoto, (clockwise from ml) Petesaloutos/Dreamstime, Darren Baker/Shutterstock, Elena Elisseeva/iStockphoto, Gustavo Caballero/Getty Images, Jaimie Duplass/iStockphoto; **52:** Amy Myers/Shutterstock; **53:** (tl) Elena Kou/Dreamstime, (tr) PhotostoGo.com, (bl) Kathy Wynn/Dreamstime, (br) Vyacheslav Osokin/Dreamstime; **54:** Michele Lugaresi/iStockphoto; **55:** Olga OSA/Shutterstock; **56:** (t) Randy Miramontez/Shutterstock, (m) Michael Nichols/National Geographic Image Collection, (b) Lisa F. Young/iStockphoto; **57:** (clockwise from t) UpperCut Images/AGE Fotostock, Jacom Stephens/iStockphoto, Steve Cole/iStockphoto, Dr. Heinz Linke/iStockphoto, Diego Cervo/Shutterstock; **58:** iStockphoto; **59:** (t) Ben Blankenburg/iStockphoto, (m) Daniel Cardiff/iStockphoto, (b) Photography Perspectives - Jeff Smith/Shutterstock; **60:** Matej Michelizza/iStockphoto; **61:** (t) Alaska Stock Images/National Geographic Image Collection, (b) Jan Rihak/iStockphoto; **62:** David Combes/Dreamstime; **63:** Claude Dagenais/iStockphoto; **64:** William Albert Allard/National Geographic Image Collection; **65:** (t) Melissa Farlow/National Geographic Image Collection, (b) William Albert Allard/National Geographic Image Collection; **66:** Sculpies/Dreamstime; **67:** (t) Yobro10/Dreamstime, (b) Zhang Bo/iStockphoto; **68:** (clockwise from tl) iStockphoto, Stepanov/Shutterstock, Galina Barskaya/iStockphoto, Kurhan/Shutterstock, (m) Elena Elisseeva/Shutterstock, (b) Dawn Liljenquist/iStockphoto; **69:** Dmitry Ersler/Dreamstime; **70:** James P. Blair/National Geographic Image Collection; **72:** Steve Shepard/iStockphoto; **73:** (both) NASA; **74:** (t) Blend Images/JupiterImages, (m) Carl Durocher/Dreamstime, (b) Jacom Stephens/iStockphoto; **75:** (t) NASA, (b) Chih-Feng Chen/iStockphoto; **76:** Tramonto/AGE Fotostock; **77:** Alexander Fediachov/iStockphoto; **78:** NASA.

PEOPLE AND PLACES UNIT 1

Lesson A

A. Complete the sentences with the correct form of the words in the box.

inhabit	employment	political	herding	migration
occur	ancient	hunting	sail	fishing

1. Christopher Columbus _____ from Europe to America for the first time in 1492.

2. Many people go to other countries for _____ because there aren't enough jobs in their home country.

3. In _____ times, people traveled by walking.

4. Some people in Central Asia still live today by _____ cows, sheep, and camels.

5. _____ is very important in Japan because people there eat a lot of seafood.

6. The first people who _____ North America came from Asia.

7. My grandfather came to this country for _____ reasons. He disagreed with the government in his old country, so he had many problems there.

8. Today, some people still enjoy _____ as a sport. They like to eat the meat from the animals that they kill.

9. Wars often cause _____ of large groups of people who need a safer place to live.

10. The accident _____ late at night on Wednesday.

B. Write questions and answers with the present perfect continuous tense.

1. (Nita/live in this city) **How long has Nita been living in this city?**
   (1992) **She's been living here since 1992.**

2. (Alan/travel overseas) _____
   (June) _____

3. (Casey/play his computer game) _____
   (six hours) _____

4. (your sister/look for a job) _____
   (a month) _____

5. (you/study English) _____
   (?) _____

Lesson B

A. Read what these people said and circle their reasons for staying where they live. For each person, add one more reason to the list.

1. My name is Maryam and I live in Dubai. I grew up in a smaller town in another part of this country, and I came here to go to college. After I graduated, I got a job in a bank. I live with my aunt and uncle. My parents are still in my hometown, and I go back to visit them often, but I really prefer living here. There aren't many jobs in my hometown, and besides, the entertainment is so much better in Dubai—movies, restaurants, and shopping.

   (employment opportunities)   ancestors lived there   good environment
   climate   having family members nearby   other: _____

2. My name is Mi-Ja. My husband and I live in a small village in South Korea, near the city of Kwangju. We're farmers, and we grow rice, cabbage, peppers, and other vegetables. My parents were farmers, and their parents were farmers—we've been living on this land for centuries. My sons live in Kwangju, and they want us to come and live with them, but I hate city life. Here, the air is clean, and it's quiet and peaceful. And all my friends are here. What would I do in the city?

   employment opportunities   ancestors lived there   good environment
   climate   having family members nearby   other: _____

3. My name is Richard. All my life, I lived in New York City, but when I retired five years ago, I moved to Florida. I love it here! It's sunny and beautiful every day of the year—and that means I can play golf every day. Golf is my favorite thing in life. I'm not far from the ocean, and I can go to the beach any time I want. It's too bad that my children are all so far away, but they can visit me any time they want to. This is the perfect life for me!

   employment opportunities   ancestors lived there   good environment
   climate   having family members nearby   other: _____

B. Write about your reasons for staying where you live—or your reasons for moving to a new place.

_____

_____

_____

_____

_____

Lesson C

A. Label the places on the map with the type of climate there.

    a. arid   b. frigid   c. rainy   d. snowy   e. temperate   f. tropical

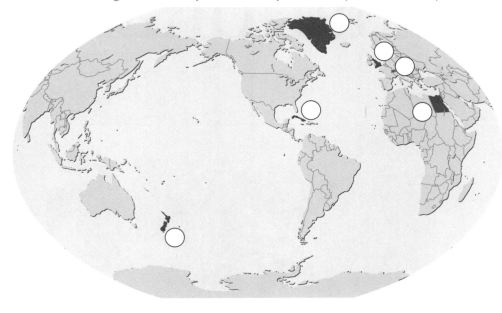

B. Write answers using *so* + adjective + *that*.

1. How old is the oldest person you've ever talked to? <u>**My grandfather is so old that he remembers the first cars in our city.**</u>
2. How rich are some movie stars? _____
3. Is it cheap or expensive to buy a house in your country? _____
4. Are you lazy or hardworking? _____
5. How good is your favorite meal? _____
6. Was this exercise easy or difficult? _____

C. Describe the place where you live. Use *so* + adjective + *that*.

1. (the weather) *It's* _____.
   It's so _____ *that* _____.
2. (the people) *They're* _____.
   They're _____.
3. (the houses) _____
   _____
4. (the streets) _____
   _____
5. (the schools) _____
   _____

Australia, the International Nation

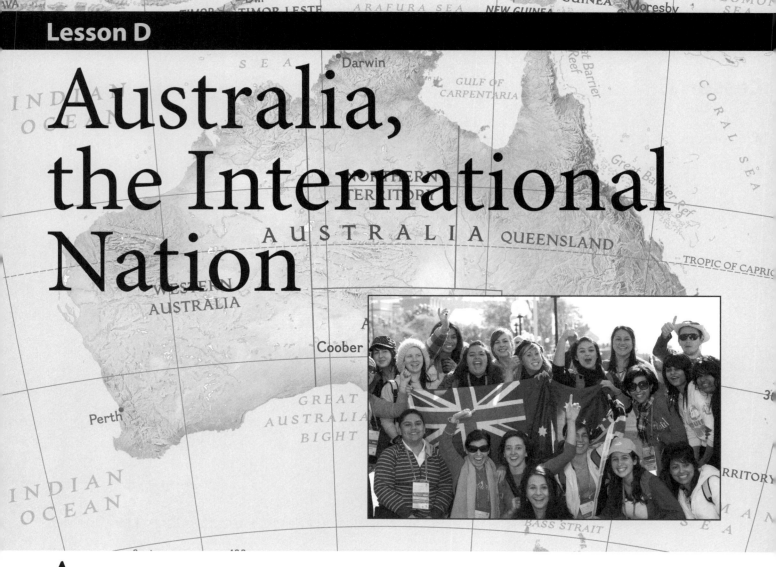

Australia is one of the most multicultural countries in the world. Almost one in every four people in Australia was born in another country: 4.8 million people out of a total population of 21 million. More than 40 percent of Australians have at least one parent who was born in another country.

In a sense, nearly all Australians are immigrants. A little more than 200 years ago, Australia was inhabited by about 350,000 native people of many different cultural groups. Then, in 1770, the explorer James Cook sailed along the coast and brought back information about the "new" land to England. In 1787, the British government started sending criminals and poor people to Australia. Later, free settlers came to Australia to start farms. In 1850, gold was discovered there, and more and more people came from Europe and China hoping to get rich. Most of them never returned home, so the population began to grow.

Australia has a huge amount of land, and in the 1940s the government decided that the best way to develop the country was to invite more settlers to come from Europe.

To attract immigrants, they offered money and other forms of help. More than 1 million people from Britain moved to Australia then, along with several hundred thousand Europeans who had lost their homes in World War II.

Migration is still growing. In 2007, more than 177,000 people went to Australia to stay permanently. Four main types of people settle there. Some go there because employment and business opportunities are better than in their home country. Others are the children, parents, or other relatives of immigrants who have become Australian citizens. A third group is refugees who are escaping from war or political problems in their home countries. Finally, there are also a few Australians who migrated to another country and now want to come home.

At the same time, Australia also sends immigrants to other countries—a smaller number. Each year, about 60,000 Australians go to live permanently in other countries. With people from so many cultures migrating in and out, Australia is truly a diverse nation.

A. Choose the correct answer.

1. The main idea of this article is ____.
   a. migration is very important in Australia
   b. Australia still needs more people
   c. the first immigrants to Australia came from Britain

2. The article talks about ____.
   a. people who migrate to Australia
   b. people who migrate from Australia
   c. both **a** and **b**

3. Which reason for migration is NOT in the article?
   a. being together with family members
   b. environmental problems
   c. employment

4. Today the number of people who are moving to Australia is ____.
   a. getting larger
   b. staying the same
   c. getting smaller

5. According to the article, ____ Australians originally came from another country.
   a. 40 percent of
   b. 167,000
   c. 4.8 million

6. The first people from outside migrated to Australia in ____.
   a. 1770
   b. 1787
   c. 1850

B. Answer the questions.

1. Which fact in the article surprised you the most?

   _____

   _____

2. Why were you surprised?

   _____

   _____

3. Why are immigrants good for a country?

   _____

   _____

4. Why are immigrants bad for a country?

   _____

   _____

C. Why do people move to your country? Why do people leave your country? Write about the reasons.

_____

_____

_____

_____

_____

_____

Review

Solve the crossword puzzle with grammar and vocabulary from this unit.

Across

3. very, very old
5. travel in a boat
6. a climate that is warm and wet
9. live in a place
10. a very cold climate
12. I ____ (study) English for five years. (3 words)
14. The climate here is ____. It rains only a few times a year.
15. a climate with a lot of rain
16. ___ places are good for skiing.
17. happen
18. killing animals for food

Down

1. related to power and the government
2. a climate that isn't very hot or very cold
4. catching fish and sea animals
7. I ____ (eat) lunch, so I'm not hungry now. (2 words)
8. caring for a group of animals
11. moving from one place to another
13. having a job

Lesson A

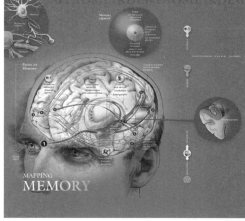

MAPPING
MEMORY

A. Complete the sentences with the correct form of the words in the box.

memorize	react	cell	retain	concentrate
visualize	portion	memory	mental	technique

1. My sister has a very good _____. She can remember hundreds of phone numbers and email addresses.

2. Please turn off the TV! I can't _____ on studying with all that noise.

3. One _____ of your brain is used for language and words.

4. When I feel stressed, I like to _____ sitting on a beautiful beach.

5. London taxi drivers have special _____ abilities to make maps in their minds.

6. Firefighters and police officers must _____ quickly in dangerous situations.

7. Your brain is made up of millions of special _____.

8. In history class last year, we _____ all the names of the presidents of our country.

9. To _____ new information in your brain, you must use it so that you don't forget it.

10. My _____ for remembering English words is to write them 10 times.

B. Complete the sentences with your own ideas. Use gerunds.

1. I remember important dates by _____.

2. _____ is a good way to meet new people.

3. I sometimes worry about _____.

4. I'm looking forward to _____ next weekend.

5. _____ is important for my country's future.

6. _____ is the best way to learn vocabulary.

C. Mr. Carter is a foreign businessman in your city. Complete the conversation with your own ideas. Use gerunds.

Mr. Carter: I'm new in your city. What's the best way to learn all the streets and places here?

You: _____

_____

Mr. Carter: I studied your language for a year, but I can't speak it very well. What's the best way to improve my speaking?

You: _____

_____

Mr. Carter: I really want to learn more about the culture of your country. What are some good ways for foreigners to do that?

You: _____

_____

Lesson B

A. Complete the chart about your senses. Use your dictionary as needed.

Sense	Verb	Body part
sight		
	smell	
touch		skin
	hear	
	taste	

B. Imagine you are the person in the pictures. What do you notice? Write one sentence for each of your senses. Use your imagination!

1. **a.** (sight) _I see ..._ _____

    b. (hearing) _____

    c. (touch) _____

    d. (smell) _____

    e. (taste) _____

2. **a.** (sight) _____

    b. (hearing) _____

    c. (touch) _____

    d. (smell) _____

    e. (taste) _____

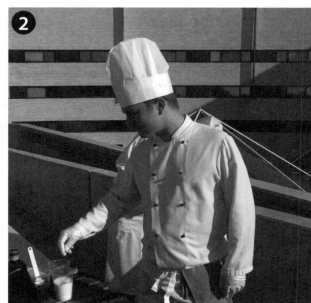

Lesson C

A. Circle the correct word to complete each sentence.

1. Dr. Awad works in a (laboratory/research) in the Medical Building at the university.
2. Jason is doing (theory/research) on how people can get over their fears.
3. Scientists have a new (theory/survey) that people learn to be afraid of snakes.
4. The class did a (survey/experiment) and asked 100 people a lot of questions.
5. In the (conclusion/experiment), the scientists gave two groups of dogs different food to eat.
6. Professor Osman talked about the (compare/results) of her research with a newspaper reporter.
7. Scientists interviewed people in different countries to (theory/compare) their feelings about snakes.
8. The (conclusion/laboratory) of the research was that people's biggest fear is accidents.

B. Dave is afraid of a lot of things. Match the words to a reason, then write sentences with *may*, *might*, or *could*.

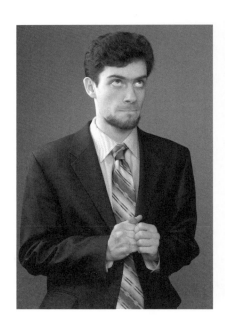

1. dogs   a. get lost
2. foreign food   b. give him a stomachache
3. visiting big cities   c. run into a shark
4. boats   d. fall in the water
5. swimming   e. have a terrible accident
6. driving   f. bite him

1. **He's afraid of dogs because they could bite him.**

2. _____

3. _____

4. _____

5. _____

6. _____

C. What are three things that make you nervous or afraid? Why? Explain using *may*, *might*, or *could*.

1. I don't like _____ because _____
   _____.

2. I'm afraid of _____ because _____
   _____.

3. _____ make(s) me nervous because _____
   _____.

The Mind-Body Connection

Norman Cousins was a famous American magazine editor. In 1964, he returned from an overseas trip and became very ill. In the hospital, he had terrible pain and couldn't move his body. Doctors told him he had a serious disease called *ankylosing spondylitis* and said he had only 1 chance in 500 of surviving. They gave him powerful drugs, but his condition only got worse.

Cousins had read about a theory that negative emotions can harm your health. He believed that positive emotions were good for your health, and he decided to try an experiment. He would fill his days with good feelings and laughter and see if that might improve his condition.

He left the hospital and moved into a hotel room. There, he got a large supply of funny TV programs and copies of old Marx Brothers movies and cartoons. He also hired a nurse to read funny stories to him. His plan was to spend the whole day laughing and thinking about happy things. On his first night in the hotel, Cousins found that laughing at the movies helped his body produce chemicals that reduced pain. For the first time in weeks, he could sleep comfortably for a few hours. Every time the pain came back, he watched another funny movie and laughed until he felt better.

Over time, Cousins was able to measure changes in his body with blood tests. He found that the harmful chemicals in his body decreased at least 5 percent every time he watched a funny movie. After a short time, he was able to stop taking all of his medications. Finally his condition improved so much that he could go back to work.

Cousins later wrote a book about how laughter and happiness helped him to survive a deadly illness. Many people didn't believe his story and said that his doctors were wrong about his disease. But since then, research has found that emotions do have a strong effect on physical health, and experiments found that laughter can help to reduce pain. Scientists today are working to understand the ways that our minds affect our bodies.

A. Circle **T** for *true*, **F** for *false*, or **NI** for *no information* (if the answer is not in the reading).

1.	Norman Cousins became ill while he was traveling in another country.	T	F	NI
2.	Doctors told Cousins that he would probably die from his disease.	T	F	NI
3.	Drugs helped to stop the pain of Cousins's disease.	T	F	NI
4.	Cousins started watching movies because he was bored.	T	F	NI
5.	Cousins spent a lot of time laughing every day.	T	F	NI
6.	Movies were better than funny stories for stopping pain.	T	F	NI
7.	When Cousins wrote his book, everyone agreed with him.	T	F	NI
8.	Scientists have done research on using laughter to stop pain.	T	F	NI

B. Number the events in order.

_____ Cousins watched funny movies and cartoons all day.

_____ Cousins went back to work.

_____ Cousins went to a hospital.

_____ Doctors told Cousins he had a terrible disease.

_____ Researchers found that Cousins's ideas were right.

_____ Cousins took many medications.

_____ The pain didn't get better.

_____ People didn't agree with Cousins's ideas.

_____ Cousins felt much better.

▲ **Norman Cousins**

C. Can your mind make your body sick or well? Write about your opinion, and give reasons and examples.

_____

_____

_____

_____

_____

_____

_____

_____

_____

_____

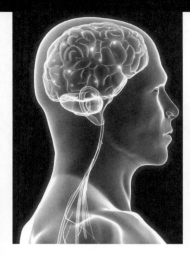

Review

Solve the crossword puzzle using grammar and vocabulary from this unit.

Across

1. I'm afraid of that dog because he __ bite me.
5. I don't like (fly) __ because airplanes make me nervous.
6. see how two things are similar or different
9. If I speak English, I __ make a mistake.
10. think very hard about something
12. If I drive there, I ____ get lost.
14. to learn exactly
16. I'm tired of (sit) __ in an office all day.

Down

1. something you decide after looking at all the information
2. make a picture in your mind
3. the sense you use your nose for
4. a place where scientists work
6. the smallest part of your body
7. a test that scientists do to see if something is true
8. I'm thinking about (become) __ a teacher.
11. a scientific idea
13. related to your mind
15. the sense you use your eyes for

Lesson A

A. Complete the article with words from the box.

oil	global warming	increase	temperature	sea level
climate change	extreme	deforestation	invasive species	conservation

Save the Planet!

- Save the forests by using wood and paper carefully. _____ is a serious problem when too many trees are cut down.
- Also, don't buy wood products from other countries. They sometimes contain _____ of insects that can harm the environment.
- Turn lights off when you aren't using them, and turn your computer off at night. _____ of electricity is important for the future.
- Drive less. An _____ in use of buses, trains, and other public transportation will help save _____.
- Think about how you affect the environment. Burning coal in electric power plants has made the earth's _____ hotter. This _____ is melting the polar ice, and the _____ in some places is getting higher. But warming isn't the only kind of _____. Many places are having more _____ weather, such as hurricanes and very cold winters.

B. Write the name of the tense in each sentence. Then rewrite the sentence in the passive voice using the same tense.

1. A famous professor wrote that book. Tense: **simple past tense**_____
   That book was written by a famous professor.

2. Bees make honey. Tense: _____
   _____

3. Our teacher will check our homework. Tense: _____
   _____

4. The police have found the lost children. Tense: _____
   _____

5. The government is building many new schools. Tense: _____
   _____

6. My mother always bakes my birthday cake. Tense: _____
   _____

7. The bad news didn't surprise me. Tense: _____
   _____

Lesson B

A. Label the types of weather.

| flood   extreme heat   drought   extreme cold   hurricane |

1. _____
2. _____
3. _____
4. _____
5. _____

B. What could be done in your school to help the environment? Complete the chart with your ideas. Use *could be*.

teaching people about the environment	1. *Posters could be made.* 2.
electricity and energy	1. 2.
garbage	1. 2.
using less paper	1. 2.

C. When a word ends in a consonant sound, and the next word begins with a vowel sound, the words are linked together. When a word ends in a consonant sound and the next word begins with the same consonant sound, the words are linked. Underline the sounds that link together. Then read the sentences out loud.

1.   I gave him my email address so he could write to me.
2.   Jim and I live very close to this school.
3.   I think hurricanes are the worst type of extreme weather.
4.   We try to learn at least ten new words every day.
5.   Do you think Cassie will invite me to her party?

Lesson C

A. Write each number in words.

1. 2,047 _____
2. 50,000,000 _____
3. 78,000 _____
4. 731,000 _____
5. 115,200 _____
6. 4,650,001 _____

B. Answer the questions. Write the numbers in words.

1. How many people live in your city? __about_____
2. What's the population of your country? _____
3. How many English words do you know? _____
4. How much does a car cost in your country? _____
5. How much does a house cost in your city? _____

C. Fill in the correct form of the verb in parentheses. Use simple past tense or past perfect tense.

1. Hana __had never spoken__ (speak, never) English before she ____went____ (go) to New York last summer.
2. I was late for class, and the teacher _____ (collect, already) the homework when I _____ (come) in.
3. The children _____ (be, not) hungry for dinner because they _____ (eat) a lot of candy after school.
4. Danny _____ (hate, always) tennis until he _____ (go) to a match last year.
5. By the time the baseball game _____ (start), the rain _____ (stop), so everyone _____ (be) happy.
6. I _____ (not, see) my friend Omar in many years when I _____ (visit) him last month.
7. My grandmother _____ (feel) very nervous when the plane _____ (take off) because she _____ (fly, never) before.

D. Write sentences about yourself using the past perfect tense.

1. By the time I was ten years old, _____
_____
2. By the time I went to bed last night, _____
_____
3. (your own idea) _____
_____

What Can One City Do?

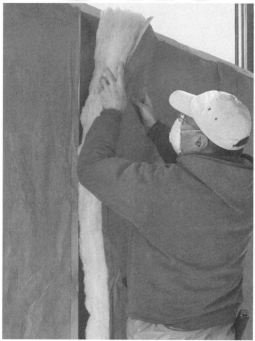

People around the world are concerned about global warming and talking about ways to stop it. The city of Cambridge, Massachusetts, in the United States, is doing more than just talking. Cambridge wants to become a world leader in energy-efficient buildings.

Today, Naema Omar is improving her 80-year-old house in Cambridge. To keep the heat inside in the winter, she is filling the space inside the walls with insulation. Insulation is usually made from chemicals, but in her house, she is using something new—insulation made from recycled blue jeans and other clothes. She has also put in a new type of light called an LED lamp that uses only a tiny amount of electricity. The lightbulbs in it last for 20 to 30 years before needing to be changed.

But eco-friendly insulation and lighting are much more expensive than the usual kind, and many people in Cambridge can't afford them. A group called Cambridge Energy Alliance (CEA) is working to solve this problem. They want to help every resident and business in the city conserve energy. People can ask the group to come and look at their house or office building. The CEA then makes a plan to save 15–30 percent on heating, gas, water, and electricity. Then the group helps people to borrow money to pay for the improvements. The money that people save by being more efficient should be enough to pay back the loan.

Ten years ago, the city of Cambridge decided to try to reduce its carbon emissions. More than 80 percent of the carbon dioxide produced in Cambridge comes from buildings—not from cars. If the program is successful, it will not only save a lot of energy but also make new jobs for local people. Workers will be needed to put in insulation, install better doors and windows, and make other energy improvements on buildings. The CEA hopes that their program will be an example for other cities.

A. Choose the correct answer.

1. Naema Omar is trying to save energy for _____.
   a. heat   b. lighting   c. both **a** and **b**

2. One problem with saving energy is that _____.
   a. it isn't always successful   b. you need money   c. you can't do it in old houses

3. The Cambridge Energy Alliance is working to save energy in _____.
   a. buildings   b. cars   c. both **a** and **b**

4. If people need money to do home energy projects, _____ helps them get it.
   a. their bank   b. the CEA   c. the government

5. The city of Cambridge wants to _____.
   a. stop producing carbon   b. help other cities   c. make efficient new houses
                                       save energy

6. Saving energy can _____.
   a. save money for people   b. make new jobs   c. both **a** and **b**

B. Number these steps in order.

_____ The Cambridge Energy Alliance makes a plan for the home.

__1__ People want to save energy in their homes.

_____ People contact the Cambridge Energy Alliance.

_____ People use the money to make energy improvements in their homes.

_____ The Cambridge Energy Alliance goes to the home.

_____ People pay back the loan with the money they save on energy.

_____ The Cambridge Energy Alliance helps people get money.

C. Write about three things that people in your country can do to save energy. Why should they do these things?

_____

_____

_____

_____

_____

_____

_____

_____

_____

Review

Solve the crossword puzzle with grammar and vocabulary from this unit.

Across

4. 1,000,000 (2 words)
6. a black liquid burned for fuel
12. how high the water in the ocean is (2 words)
13. 200 (2 words)
15. get larger
16. 600,000 (3 words)
17. very large in degree or intensity
18. That movie was made _____ two students.

Down

1. The bank _____ (rob) last night. (2 words)
2. 2,000,020 (3 words)
3. cutting down trees over a large area
5. Earth is getting hotter because of _____. (2 words)
7. Many things _____ (can, do) to save energy. (3 words)
8. 10,000 (2 words)
9. By four o'clock, I _____ (finish) all my work. (2 words)
10. saving or protecting the environment
11. how hot or cold something is
14. A lot of pollution _____ (cause) by cars. (2 words)

MONEY

Lesson A

A. Circle the correct answer to show the meaning of the vocabulary word in **bold**.

1. I **borrowed** some money from my friend because (she/I) didn't have any money.
2. You really need a **budget**. You need (a plan/a wallet) for all your money.
3. If you pay for something with **cash**, you use (coins and bills/a credit card).
4. I **lend** money to people in my family if they have (a problem/a birthday).
5. Risa is **in debt.** Every month she (pays money to the bank/gets a big salary).
6. If your **expenses** are high, you (get/spend) a lot of money.
7. Your **income** is all the money that you (pay/receive).
8. Those jeans are a real **bargain**. They're so (expensive/cheap)!

B. Answer the questions.

1. Do you ever borrow money? Why or why not? _____
   _____.

2. Do you lend money? Why or why not? _____
   _____.

3. What are your biggest expenses every month? _____
   _____.

4. What was the best bargain you ever found? _____
   _____.

C. Tomoko is a university student in Tokyo. Read what she says and complete the sentences with the correct form of the verb in parentheses—gerund or infinitive.

"I hope _____ (go) to Europe next year, so I'm trying _____ (save) enough money. Now I avoid _____ (eat) in restaurants with my friends, because that's very expensive. And I've given up _____ (go) to movies. So far, I've saved 100,000 yen—that's about $1,000—but it's not enough. I want _____ (stay) in Europe for at least one month, so I need _____ (bring) a lot more money with me. I've decided _____ (live) with my parents, because my student apartment is very expensive. And I've considered (get) _____ a part-time job. But my expenses are so high. I have to pay for my books, my cell phone, and my food. And wearing nice clothes is very important to me!"

D. What should Tomoko do? Write ideas using these verbs with a gerund or infinitive.

1. try _She should_____
2. stop _____
3. begin _____
4. continue _____

Lesson B

A. Read the article and answer the questions with information from the article and your own ideas.

> **The Value of Gold**
> There are three reasons why gold is so valuable. First, it is beautiful. People in almost every culture have used it in jewelry and works of art. Second, it is useful. It carries electricity well, and many electronic devices like computers and cell phones contain small amounts of gold. Finally, it is scarce. It is found in only a few places in the world, and often thousands of kilograms of rocks must be processed to find just a few grams of gold. For these reasons, the price of gold is always high.

1. Why is gold valuable? _____, _____,
   _____.

2. Do people in your country think gold is valuable? _____

3. In your opinion, is gold the most valuable thing in the world? Explain your answer.
   _____
   _____

B. Think about the three most valuable things you have and list them here (for example, *my camera* or *a picture of my grandmother*). Then check the reasons why each thing is valuable for you.

	Item #1: _____	Item #2: _____	Item #3: _____
a. It cost a lot of money.			
b. It's important in my life.			
c. It's very useful.			
d. It came from someone I love.			
e. It's very old.			
f. It's unusual.			
g. Many people want to have this.			
h. other reasons (write the reasons)			

C. Write about one of the items in exercise **B.** Describe it and explain why it's valuable to you.

_____
_____
_____
_____

Lesson C

A. Match the banking terms with their meanings.

1. savings account ____
2. teller ____
3. PIN number ____
4. deposit ____
5. receipt ____
6. ATM ____
7. checking account ____
8. withdraw ____

a. a paper that tells how much money you got or spent
b. a bank account where you keep money to spend later
c. put money into the bank
d. take money out of the bank
e. a person who works in a bank
f. a bank account that you can use to pay for things
g. a secret number that you use with a bank machine
h. a bank machine

B. Fill in the correct form of the verb, active or passive. Use the correct tense.

1. Today, ATMs _____ (find) in countries around the world.
2. The money _____ (steal) from the bank yesterday by two men. The police _____ (find) them one hour later.
3. That TV program _____ (watch) by more then 5 million people last night.
4. In the past, credit cards _____ (use) only by adults. Now, in some countries, teenagers _____ (get) them.
5. My graduation dinner last week _____ (cook) by my mother. My sister _____ (make) my celebration cake.

C. Make each sentence passive. Form the correct tense with *be*.

1. George cuts her hair. _____
2. George cut her hair yesterday. _____
3. George is going to cut her hair. _____
4. George will cut her hair. _____
5. George might cut her hair. _____

D. Circle the agent in each sentence. If the agent is not needed, rewrite the sentence without it.

1. The first coins were made by people in Turkey 3,000 years ago.

   _____

2. Many flowers for perfume are grown in France by farmers.

   _____

3. The Mona Lisa was painted by Leonardo da Vinci.

   _____

4. Some very good cars are produced by workers in Korea.

   _____

5. I was surprised to hear that those paintings were made by children.

   _____

Banknotes: Facts about Paper Money

The first kinds of money used in different countries were gold, silver, and other valuable things. But before long, new kinds of money were needed. There wasn't enough metal to make coins, and people had trouble buying things. In addition, coins were difficult to carry around—especially for rich people in China. The coins there had a hole in the middle, and people put a string through the coins. These long strings of coins were extremely heavy.

In about 600 AD, Chinese merchants found a solution to these problems. The merchants would leave their strings of coins with a government official and get a piece of paper that said how many strings of coins they had left there. They could use this paper to buy things from a seller, and the seller could take the paper to get the coins. These papers were the first banknotes, or paper money.

By about 960 AD, the government of China was printing pictures on paper to make official banknotes. The first paper money was used in Europe in 1574, when banks in Holland made very small paper "coins". Sweden printed the first banknotes in Europe in 1660.

Today, countries around the world have their own banknotes. Large countries print their own banknotes, and a company in England called De La Rue prints banknotes for many smaller countries like Honduras, Sri Lanka, and Fiji. Most banknotes are still printed on very heavy paper, but some countries, like Australia, use very thin plastic. Because it's easy to make false banknotes, countries put many special features in their banknotes. They use ink that changes color, metal threads in the paper, and even plastic windows in the money. These make the banknotes difficult to copy.

But there is still one big problem with banknotes that hasn't been solved. Metal coins last for a long time, but banknotes quickly become dirty and wear out. An average banknote lasts only a few years. In the United States, old banknotes are collected by the government, cut in small pieces, and recycled into other paper products. In Australia, the plastic banknotes are melted and made into garbage cans!

A. Circle **T** for *true*, **F** for *false*, or **NI** for *no information* (if the answer isn't in the reading).

1. Coins were made before banknotes.   T   F   NI
2. Banknotes don't last as long as metal coins.   T   F   NI
3. Some people don't like to use banknotes.   T   F   NI
4. *Banknote* is another name for paper money.   T   F   NI
5. Old banknotes can be recycled and made
   into new things.   T   F   NI
6. Sweden made the first banknotes in the world.   T   F   NI
7. People don't make as many false banknotes now
   because they are difficult to copy.   T   F   NI
8. Banknotes were invented in 1574.   T   F   NI

B. Answer the questions.

Which country/countries in the article . . .

1. had the first banknotes in Europe? _____
2. has a company that prints banknotes for other countries? _____
3. makes garbage cans from old money? _____
4. had the first paper money? _____
5. made coins from paper? _____
6. don't print their own money? _____
7. makes old money into paper products? _____

C. What picture is on the smallest banknote in your country? Why was that picture used?
Imagine your country wants to make a new banknote. What picture should be on it? Explain your reasons.

_____
_____
_____
_____
_____
_____
_____
_____
_____

Review

Solve the crossword puzzle with grammar and vocabulary from this unit.

Across

5. a bank account where you keep money to spend later (2 words)
9. money that you spend
10. give money to someone who will pay you back later
12. a plan for spending money
13. a bank machine
15. a person who works in a bank
16. take money out of the bank

Down

1. secret number for a bank machine (2 words)
2. something cheap that you buy
3. get money that you will give back later
4. money that you receive for working
6. Credit cards ____ (use) around the world today. (2 words)
7. The first coins ____ (make) in Turkey. (2 words)
8. owing money to a bank or a company (2 words)
11. put money in the bank
14. coins and paper money

Lesson A

A. Match the words with their meanings.

1. emergency _____
2. panic _____
3. natural disaster _____
4. preparation _____
5. supplies _____
6. equipment _____
7. evacuate _____
8. first aid _____
9. cope with _____
10. situation _____

a. all the things that are happening at one time
b. food, clothes, and other things needed for daily life
c. an accident caused by nature, like an earthquake
d. leave your house because of danger
e. tools that you need to do something
f. a dangerous time
g. simple medical treatment
h. getting ready before doing something
i. succeed in dealing with a problem
j. become very afraid

B. Write sentences about these unreal conditions and results.

1. condition: I/see an accident __ result: I/call for help
   If I saw an accident, I would call for help.

2. condition: we/know first aid __ result: we/help a lot of people

   _____

3. result: I/visit my grandparents more often __ condition: I/have more time

   _____

4. condition: he/not know how to swim __ result: he/be afraid of water

   _____

5. result: I/not give any homework __ condition: I/be the teacher of this class

   _____

C. Look at these unreal situations. Write sentences about what you would do in each one.

1. _____
2. _____
3. _____
4. _____

Lesson B

Read the survival situations. Write the possible results of each plan. Then choose the best plan and write your reasons.

Situation 1: You are walking in a dark street at night in your city. A man steps up to you and says, "Give me all your money!" His hands are in his pockets. You can't see if he is holding anything. You have about $20 in your wallet.

Plan	Possible results
1. Run away.	The man might catch me, and then I would have a bigger problem.
2. Give the man your money.	
3. Shout, "Help me! Help me!"	
4. Say, "I don't have any money."	
5. (your own idea)	
The best plan is number _____. Reasons:	

Situation 2: You are on vacation in the mountains, 50 kilometers from the nearest town. Your car goes off the road. The weather is very cold but sunny. You are not hurt, but your car can't be driven. Very few people travel on this road. You have food and water for two days.

Plan	Possible results
1. Stay inside your car and wait for people to find you.	
2. Take the food and water with you. Start walking to the town.	
3. Build a big fire outside the car so that people can find you.	
4. Eat the food and drink the water. Then walk to a bigger road.	
5. (your own idea)	
The best plan is number _____. Reasons:	

Lesson C

A. Match the words with their meanings.

1. species _____
2. ban _____
3. reserve _____
4. preservation _____
5. ecosystem _____
6. predatory _____
7. restore _____
8. endangered _____

a. bring back into good condition
b. all the plants and animals that live in a particular place
c. a place where hunting and fishing are not allowed
d. might all die
e. hunting and killing other animals for food
f. a scientific word for a kind of plant or animal
g. keeping something in good condition
h. not allowing something

B. Write sentences with *wish*.

1. Rachel failed the test. **She wishes she had passed the test.** _____
2. My city doesn't have any parks. _____
3. Josh lives far from his school. _____
4. I don't have a lot of friends. _____
5. I'm not sitting on the beach now. _____
6. Katie spent a lot of money last week. _____
7. I have to wash the dishes every day. _____

C. John is unhappy about his life. Write sentences about his wishes.

1. He wishes _____
_____
2. _____
_____
3. _____
_____
4. _____
_____
5. (your own idea) _____
_____

D. Write your own wishes about these things.

1. (Your city) I _____
2. (Your country) _____
3. (The world) _____

Ready for Anything

Every day, newspapers are filled with articles about natural disasters like floods, earthquakes, and hurricanes. These emergencies can occur in every country in the world, so it's important to be ready for them. There are three important things you should do at home to prepare.

First, stock up on emergency supplies. You should keep enough food and water for at least three days in your house. Choose food that can be stored for a long time and food that can be eaten without cooking. Canned foods such as soup, fish, meat, and fruit are good choices. You can also store dry foods like crackers and cookies. Be sure to store food that you like and include a few special treats like candy or nuts. In an emergency situation, it's nice to have something to cheer you up. If you have babies, small children, or elderly people in your family, remember to include any special foods that they need. And be sure to keep plenty of water. Each person needs 1 gallon (4 liters) of water per day for drinking and basic washing.

In addition, think about equipment you might need for the kinds of disasters that happen in your country. You might need blankets, very warm clothes, flashlights, or plastic bags. Think about possible situations, and buy the things that would be needed.

Finally, plan what you will do in case you need to evacuate your home. Decide where you will go. It's good to arrange a meeting place in advance—such as a relative's home or a big public building. Also, plan a way to contact other family members if you become separated. Be sure that all family members know the phone number of a contact person in another city.

People don't like to think about natural disasters, but a little bit of preparation can save lives. Following these steps will help you be ready for any kind of emergency.

A. Complete the outline with information from the reading.

Ready for Anything

I. Natural disasters happen every day.

    Examples: _____, _____,

        _____

People should prepare at home for disasters.

  II. Three steps to prepare for disasters

    A. _____

      1. canned foods

        examples: _____, _____, _____,

          _____

      2. _____

        examples: crackers, cookies

      3. treats

        examples: _____, _____

      4. water

        _____ for each person for each day

B. _____

  examples: blankets, very warm clothes, flashlights, or plastic bags

C. _____

  a. decide _____

  b. plan _____

III. Conclusion

  A. People don't _____

  B. Preparing _____

B. What is the most common emergency situation in your country?
Write about what you would do if it happened to you.

_____

_____

_____

_____

_____

_____

Review

Solve the crossword puzzle with grammar and vocabulary from this unit.

Across

5. simple medical help (2 words)
7. a time when your life is in danger
10. If I had time, I _____ (go) to visit my sister in London. (2 words)
12. become very afraid
13. tools you need to do something
14. put something back into good condition
17. keeping something in good condition
18. leave your house because of danger

Down

1. one kind of plant or animal
2. Floods are a common natural _____ in my country.
3. things you need for everyday life
4. getting ready for something
6. Jack wishes he _____ (not have) to get up early. (2 words)
8. I wish I _____ (can speak) Chinese. (2 words)
9. I wish I _____ (be) rich!
11. all the plants and animals in a place
15. not allowed
16. If you _____ with a bad situation, you get through it successfully.

Lesson A

A. Complete the article with words from the box. Use the correct form.

technique	style	decorate	design
represent	realistic	express	abstract

The Art of the Carpet

Weavers in Iran make beautiful carpets. The _____ is simple, but it takes many years to learn: the weavers tie many small knots, and each knot is a different color. Each city uses a different _____ with different colors. Some of these designs are _____ such as flowers and fountains. Other designs are _____ using only colored shapes. But these shapes are also symbols. For example, a big square might _____ a garden. The colors _____ feelings like peace and hope. Carpets are made in other countries in Asia and the Middle East, including Turkey and Pakistan, and each country has its own special _____. People around the world use these beautiful carpets to _____ their homes.

B. Write what each person said. Use reported speech and make all the necessary changes.

1. Nawal: "I have a headache." **Nawal said she had a headache.** _____

2. Rita: "I live in New York." _____

3. The president: "I have a plan to help our country."

   _____

4. Mohammed: "I can't go out because I'm doing my homework."

   _____

5. Cathy: "I haven't been to the new museum."

   _____

6. Chris and Dennis: "We really like living here."

   _____

7. Emily: "I'm going to my hometown tomorrow."

   _____

8. Your friend: "_____"

   _____

C. Think of a very important phone call that you had. What did the other person say? Write three sentences in reported speech.

1. _____

2. _____

3. _____

Lesson B

A. Look at each painting and write your ideas.

Painting 1

1. Describe the painting. _____
   _____

2. Think of a title for this painting. "_____"
3. Where is a good place to put this painting? Why? _____
   _____

Painting 2

1. Describe the painting. _____
   _____

2. Think of a title for this painting. "_____"
3. Where is a good place to put this painting? Why? _____
   _____

Painting 3

1. Describe the painting. _____
   _____

2. Think of a title for this painting. "_____"
3. Where is a good place to put this painting? Why? _____
   _____

Painting 4

1. Describe the painting. _____
   _____

2. Think of a title for this painting. "_____"
3. Where is a good place to put this painting? Why? _____
   _____

B. Answer the questions.

1. Which painting do you like the most? Why? _____
   _____

2. Which painting do you like the least? Why? _____
   _____

Lesson C

A. Look at the picture. Write each item in the correct box. Then add one more idea to each box.

brass	leather	straw	stone
vase			

wood	bamboo	gold	clay

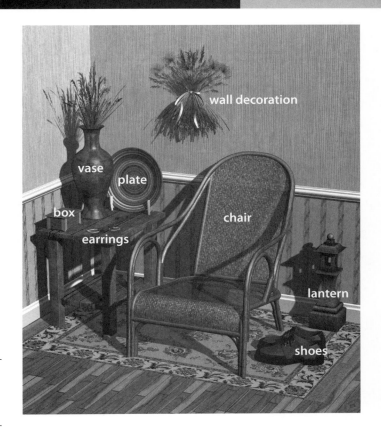

B. Combine the two sentences by using an adjective clause. Use *who* or *that*.

1. Sandy has a friend.
   The friend makes metal sculptures.
   Sandy has a friend who makes metal sculptures.

2. I want to get a cheap camera.
   The camera takes good pictures.
   _____

3. The dictionary is on the table.
   The dictionary is mine.
   _____

4. I read a great book.
   The book was written by a 16-year-old girl.
   _____

5. I know a doctor.
   The doctor works with elderly people.
   _____

6. Sanjay likes paintings.
   The paintings have a lot of bright colors.
   _____

C. Write sentences with adjective clauses about kinds of things you like/dislike/enjoy/hate/love.

1. music __I like music that_____
2. books _____
3. art _____
4. food _____

Biographies of Great Artists:
Frida Kahlo

Self portrait with Changuito, 1945. (left)

The two Fridas, 1939. (right)

Frida Kahlo was born in Mexico in 1907. As a small child, she was very happy and ran and laughed all the time—even in church. When she was six years old, her life changed completely. She got a serious disease called polio, and had to <u>remain</u> in bed for nine months. The disease made her left leg shorter than her right, and she had serious problems walking.

When Frida was 15, she was enrolled at a prestigious school in Mexico City. There she was influenced by the modern changes that were <u>sweeping</u> across Mexico. She cut her hair short like a boy and started riding a bicycle—shocking for a young woman of her time. She was very interested in science, and decided to become a doctor.

Then, in September 1925, Frida was involved in a <u>horrendous</u> accident. She was riding on a bus when it crashed into a trolley car. Her right leg was broken in 11 places, and she had many other broken bones. For the rest of her life, she had <u>severe</u> pain every day caused by that accident. She had to give up her plans to become a doctor, because she knew she would never be strong enough. While lying in bed after the accident, Frida began reading books about art. Her father was a painter and photographer, and he <u>encouraged</u> her interest in art. One year later, she completed her first painting: a portrait of herself.

Over the years, Frida Kahlo painted more than 200 pictures. Most of them were about very personal subjects—her health and her dreams. She also used many bright colors and symbols from Mexican culture. Frida married the famous Mexican artist Diego Rivera, and they had a very difficult marriage, but she continued to paint, even after her health started failing. When a famous gallery wanted to have a show of her work, her bed was carried into the gallery so that she could talk to visitors.

Frida died in 1954, at the age of 47, but her paintings still fascinate people. In 2002, a popular movie was made of her life.

El Camion (The Bus), 1929.

A. Look at the underlined words in the reading and try to guess their meanings. Match them to the definitions.

1. biographies ____
2. remain ____
3. sweeping ____
4. horrendous ____
5. severe ____
6. encourage ____

a. extremely bad
b. moving very fast
c. very strong
d. stay
e. support and help
f. stories of people's lives

B. Circle **T** for *true* or **F** for *false*.

1. Frida Kahlo had a happy childhood until she was six. T F
2. As a teenager, Frida liked modern ideas. T F
3. Frida became a doctor. T F
4. Frida began painting after she suffered a terrible accident. T F
5. Frida's father and husband were artists too. T F
6. All of Frida's paintings were about Mexican culture. T F
7. Frida had to stop painting when her health became worse. T F
8. Frida died when she was still young. T F

C. Choose one of the paintings on the previous page and describe it. Do you like it? Explain your reasons.

_____
_____
_____
_____
_____
_____
_____
_____
_____

Review

Solve the crossword puzzle with
vocabulary and grammar from this unit.

Across

2. That box is made of ____. It grows in warm places.
6. I want a painting ____ makes me smile.
9. Those shoes are made of ____.
10. show your feelings about something
12. That table is made of ____ from a tropical tree.
13. a way to do something
14. Those sandals are made of ____. It's a kind of dead plant.
16. That sculpture is made of ____. It's very heavy.
17. That pot is made of ____.
18. a way of making art that is used by one artist

Down

1. art made with only shapes and lines
3. That bowl is made of ____. It's a shiny metal.
4. a very expensive metal
5. She said he ____ (win) a prize for his art. (2 words)
7. art that looks like something real
8. be a symbol for something
11. make something more beautiful
15. I know an artist ____ makes big sculptures.

Lesson A

A. Complete the sentences with the correct form of the words in the box.

passenger	increase	directly	destination	reduce
pilot	freight	speed	efficient	fuel

1. The new planes are very large. They can carry more than 700 _____.
2. This flight doesn't make any stops. It goes _____ from Singapore to London.
3. Today, long-distance flights have several _____. One of them flies the plane while the others are resting.
4. Five years ago, the number of tourists in our city was 200,000. Last year, that number _____ to more than 400,000.
5. It's very expensive to send heavy _____ on a plane. It's much cheaper by ship.
6. Plane tickets are more expensive now because the cost of _____ for the airplanes has gone up.
7. My car is very _____. It doesn't use a lot of gasoline.
8. The _____ of flight 972 is Buenos Aires.
9. Most airplanes fly at a _____ of more than 600 kilometers per hour.
10. Faster planes will _____ the time it takes to travel from Australia to Europe.

B. Write passive sentences with the present perfect tense about these developments in transportation.

1. smaller, more efficient cars/design <u>Smaller and more efficient cars have been designed.</u>
2. new kinds of fuel from plants/test _____
3. faster public transportation/plan _____
4. electric buses/develop _____
5. cars that use hydrogen/invent _____

C. Read the mayor's speech. Complete the passive sentences with the present continuous tense.

Our city's transportation future ___<u>is being planned</u>___ (plan) right now. To connect us with the world, a larger airport _____ (build). Work _____ (start) on a new subway system. We have already bought hundreds of new, modern buses and they _____ (use) by our citizens every day. And changes _____ (made) in our street system to make traffic flow better. Every day, our transportation system _____ (improve) so that the people of our city will be able to get around more quickly and comfortably.

Lesson B

A. Read the information.

National University is very crowded, so a new campus is being built 20 miles (30 kilometers) outside the city. Nearly all of the 20,000 students live in the city. Now there is only one small road between the city and the new campus. People have written letters to the editor about different plans for solving the transportation problem.

> The solution is simple: build a big expressway to the new campus. If 20,000 students try to drive on that small road, it will be a traffic jam all day. An expressway would cost $20 million, but other people will use it too. The city could expand, and be less crowded.

> I think the government should lend money to students to buy cheap cars. That would be good for the economy, because car dealers will sell a lot of cars. It will also be good for the students, because they will have the freedom to come and go whenever they want.

> The best idea is to build a subway line to the campus. It's true that this will take five years and cost $30 million, but subways are the fastest and most comfortable way to get around. Students work hard—we should try to make their lives easier!

> The quickest and best solution is to start a bus system from the old campus to the new campus. It's much less expensive than other plans, and we could start today. Buses aren't as fast as cars, but they save a lot of energy. Besides, students could do their homework on the bus.

B. Complete the chart with information from the letters to the editor and your own ideas.

build an expressway	Advantages: Disadvantages:
lend money for cars	Advantages: Disadvantages:
build a subway	Advantages: Disadvantages:
start a bus system	Advantages: Disadvantages:

C. In your opinion, which is the best plan? Explain your reasons.

_____

_____

_____

_____

_____

Lesson C

A. Match these public transportation words with their meanings.

1. board ___   a. get on a bus, train, or subway
2. pass ___   b. the place where a bus or train line ends
3. ticket ___   c. the money they you pay to use public transportation once
4. fare ___   d. come together
5. route ___   e. a card that lets you use public transportation for a week or a month
6. transfer ___   f. the way between two places that a bus or train travels
7. connect ___   g. change from one bus or train to another
8. terminal ___   h. a paper that lets you use public transportation once

B. Rewrite these questions to make them more polite.

1. Where is the director's office? (can you tell me)

   _____

2. What time is it? (do you know)

   _____

3. When will the doctor see me? (I'd like to know)

   _____

4. Can I use my cell phone here? (could you please tell me)

   _____

5. Is there a post office near here? (do you know)

   _____

C. Complete the conversation with polite questions.

Beth: Excuse me. I want to go to the Louvre Museum. _____?

Sylvie: Yes. From here, you take the subway to the Pont Neuf station. You have to transfer at Chatelet station.

Beth: _____ is close to the museum?

Sylvie: Yes, it's very close to the museum. You only have to walk for a few minutes.

Beth: _____?

Sylvie: I think it costs 1 euro, but I'm not sure.

Beth: And—sorry! I have one more question. _____?

Sylvie: You can buy tickets from the machines. They're right by the entrance of the subway station.

Beth: Thanks so much for your help.

Sylvie: You're welcome. Enjoy your visit.

Streets for People

Walking is the oldest way of getting around—and still one of the most important. For short distances, for exercise, or just for fun, walking is much better than driving or riding. But in many cities today, walking can also be dangerous. Cars and trucks pass much too close to pedestrians, and there are frequent accidents.

A man from Brisbane, Australia, named David Engwicht wants to do something about this. His book *Reclaiming Our Cities and Towns* has a simple message: We need to take back our streets and make them better for walking.

In the past, Engwicht says, streets belonged to everybody. Kids played there, and people walked to work or shops. Now, however, streets are designed only for cars and trucks. People stay inside to get away from the noise and dangerous traffic, and lose contact with their neighbors. Engwicht believes that people need to take back their streets.

This process is happening already in cities around the world. Neighbors in the city of Delft, in the Netherlands, took action against dangerous traffic on their street. They put old couches, tables, and other furniture in the street. Cars could still pass, but they had to drive very slowly. When the police arrived, they saw that these <u>illegal</u> actions were actually making the streets safer. Soon city officials started planning ways to make cars slow down and "<u>calm</u>" the traffic.

In many different countries, people are speaking up and working hard to make their cities safer and more pleasant for <u>pedestrians</u>. Cities have painted <u>crosswalks</u> on their streets, made streets narrower, put in traffic lights and <u>bicycle lanes</u>, and made plans to help more kids walk or bike to school.

Engwicht travels around the world, helping people think differently about pedestrians, streets, and neighborhoods. Besides his books and articles, he gives many speeches. He has worked in neighborhoods from Honolulu to Scotland.

Engwicht says we should think about streets as our "outdoor living room." Calming the traffic is just the beginning. In the future, streets will be safe places for children again, and walking will be more practical—and more fun.

A. Find the underlined words in the reading with these meanings.

1. a place where people can walk across a street safely _____

2. people who are walking _____

3. make something more slow and careful _____

4. a part of the street only for bicycles _____

5. against the law _____

B. Circle **T** for *true* or **F** for *false*.

1. David Engwicht wrote a book about why walking is healthy.   T   F
2. David Engwicht thinks that people are more important than cars.   T   F
3. The people in Delft made it easier for pedestrians to use the streets.   T   F
4. The police in Delft didn't like the changes in the street.   T   F
5. Many cities are trying to make streets better for pedestrians.   T   F

C. What would Engwicht think about these ideas?

1. make special streets only for pedestrians

   good idea   bad idea

2. form groups for children to walk to school together

   good idea   bad idea

3. build wider streets

   good idea   bad idea

4. make cars drive slower on all city streets

   good idea   bad idea

5. put more parking lots in the city

   good idea   bad idea

D. Write about walking in your city. Is it a good place for walking? Why, or why not? How many people walk there? What changes would make your city better for walking?

_____

_____

_____

_____

_____

Review

Solve the crossword puzzle with vocabulary and grammar from this unit.

Across

2. the place where a bus or train is going
3. The ___ for the subway is $1.
5. a person who is traveling on a train, bus, etc.
7. Electric cars (make) _____ today. (3 words)
9. things that are transported on a vehicle
10. (know) _____ how much a ticket costs? (3 words)
14. change from one bus or train to another
15. (tell) _____ me where the bus stop is? (3 words)
16. how fast you are going
17. a substance like gasoline or oil

Down

1. Three new airports (build) _____ in the last 10 years. (3 words)
4. the way a bus or train goes to a place
5. a person whose job is flying airplanes
6. the end of a bus or train line
8. without stopping
11. get larger
12. A bus ___ for one month costs $20.
13. get on a plane or train

Lesson A

A. Complete the sentences with the correct form of the words in the box.

athlete	match	training	cheat
sportsmanship	winner	loser	team

1. At the Olympics, individual _____ from every country in the world come together to compete.
2. Yoshi plays on his university's soccer _____.
3. Some of the runners stopped to help another runner when she fell during the race. That's an example of good _____!
4. At the Olympics, the three _____ in each competition get medals.
5. It was a very exciting tennis _____. Both of the women played really well.
6. Athletes need many years of _____ before they can compete in the Olympics.
7. One player tried to _____ during the golf competition. He moved the ball when no one was looking at him.
8. I was the _____ in the big tennis match, so I decided to practice harder every week.

B. Complete the conversations with the negative questions.

1. _____
   Yes, I am. I started work at 4:00 a.m. today.
2. _____
   No. She's actually a doctor.
3. _____
   No, not really. It's too sweet for me.
4. _____
   No, I'm not. I want to stay home and have a quiet evening.
5. _____
   Yes. I'll talk to them tonight.
6. _____
   Yes, I do. I'm really hungry!

Shouldn't you call your parents?

Aren't you tired?

Don't you want to have dinner?

Isn't your friend a nurse?

Don't you like chocolate?

Aren't you going to the party?

C. Answer these negative questions.

1. Aren't you American? _____
2. Weren't you late for class yesterday? _____
3. Don't you like sports? _____
4. Shouldn't you save more money? _____

Lesson B

A. Unscramble the names of sports.

1. bbaallse _____
2. tindabnom _____
3. intsne _____
4. inskig _____
5. ratmila star _____
6. ofgl _____
7. erccos _____
8. glicybinc _____
9. lolelylavb _____
10. noxbig _____
11. skallbetab _____
12. wgmismin _____

B. Read these people's answers on the questionnaire. Then choose the best sport for each one, and explain your reasons.

Sport Preference Questionnaire

Name: **Danny Santos**

1. Which kinds of exercise do you prefer—vigorous or gentle? **Both kinds are OK. But I want to play a sport to help me relax after classes.**
2. Are you an introvert or an extrovert? **It depends. I like to spend time with a few good friends, but I also like to be alone a lot.**
3. Are you a perfectionist? **Yes, but I try not to get upset when I make a mistake.**
4. Are you very focused when you do things? **I have to be very focused—I'm a chemistry major at the university.**
5. Do you like to do one thing, or do you prefer a lot of change? **I prefer to do one thing at a time.**

The best sport for Danny is _____.

Reasons: _____

_____

_____

_____

Sport Preference Questionnaire

Name: **LaKeisha Green**

1. Which kinds of exercise do you prefer—vigorous or gentle? **I sit at a desk all day at work, so I like to really move during my free time!**
2. Are you an introvert or an extrovert? **Definitely an extrovert. I get bored when I'm alone.**
3. Are you a perfectionist? **Not really. And when I play sports, I want to have fun.**
4. Are you very focused when you do things? **I can be when I'm at work. But it's nice to have a break from that.**
5. Do you like to do one thing, or do you prefer a lot of change? **I really like to do a lot of different things.**

The best sport for LaKeisha is _____.

Reasons: _____

_____

_____

_____

Lesson C

A. Read the newspaper article and fill in the spaces with words from the box.

league
points
coach
championship
score
medal
trophy
scoreboard

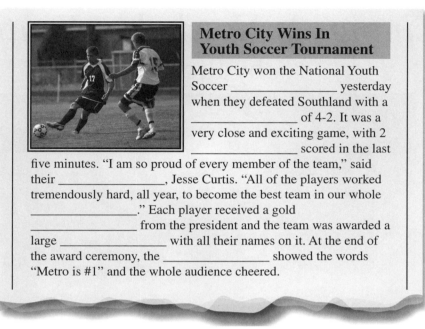

Metro City Wins In Youth Soccer Tournament

Metro City won the National Youth Soccer _____ yesterday when they defeated Southland with a _____ of 4-2. It was a very close and exciting game, with 2 _____ scored in the last five minutes. "I am so proud of every member of the team," said their _____, Jesse Curtis. "All of the players worked tremendously hard, all year, to become the best team in our whole _____." Each player received a gold _____ from the president and the team was awarded a large _____ with all their names on it. At the end of the award ceremony, the _____ showed the words "Metro is #1" and the whole audience cheered.

B. Fill in a relative pronoun in each sentence.

1. The man _____ I met at the party is from South Africa.
2. Did you eat the cake _____ I brought home?
3. The book _____ we had to read for our class was 400 pages long!
4. The actor _____ I like the most is Matt Damon.
5. My mother really enjoyed the presents _____ we gave her.

C. Combine the two sentences by writing an adjective clause.

1. He bought a car. The car was very expensive.
   **The car that he bought was very expensive.**

2. We watched a movie. The movie was more than three hours long.
   _____

3. The teacher asked me a question. I couldn't answer the question.
   _____

4. He told me the news. The news was good.
   _____

5. I saw the thieves. The thieves were wearing black clothes.
   _____

6. You lent me the CD. The CD was great.
   _____

7. We watched the tennis match on TV. The tennis match wasn't very exciting.
   _____

Voice Your Opinion:
Change Is Needed in Youth Sports
by Richard Wade

Everywhere you look, you see kids bouncing a basketball or waving a tennis racquet. And these kids are getting younger and younger. In this country, children can compete on basketball, baseball, and volleyball teams starting at age nine. The youth soccer organization has teams for children as young as five. And swimming and gymnastics classes begin at age four, to prepare children for competition.

It's true that a few of these kids will develop into highly skilled athletes and may even become members of our national Olympic teams. But what about the others, the average kids? This emphasis on competition in sports is having serious negative effects.

Children who get involved in competitive sports at a young age often grow tired of their sport. Many parents pressure their kids to choose one sport and devote all their time to it. A survey found that 79 percent of parents of young athletes wanted their children to concentrate on one sport. But 66 percent of the young athletes wanted to play more than one sport—for fun.

Another problem is the pressure imposed by over-competitive parents and coaches. Children are not naturally competitive. In fact, a recent study by Paulo David found that most children don't even understand the idea of competition until they are seven years old. Very young kids don't know why their parents are pushing them so hard.

The third, and biggest, problem for young athletes is the lack of time to do their homework, have fun, be with friends—in short, time to be kids. When they are forced to spend every afternoon at sports practice, they often start to hate their chosen sport. Researchers found that 70 percent of kids who take part in competitive sports before the age of twelve quit before they turn eighteen. Many of them completely lose interest in sports. Excessive competition takes away all the enjoyment.

We need to remember the purpose of youth sports—to give kids a chance to have fun while developing strong, healthy bodies.

A. What is the main idea of this reading?

    a. many children in this country spend too much time playing sports

    b. sports for children have two important purposes

    c. too much competition is not good for children

B. Find the information in the reading.

1. The age when children can start these sports:
   a. swimming _____
   b. soccer _____
   c. basketball _____
   d. gymnastics _____
2. The number of children who want to play more than one sport: _____ percent
3. The number of children who stop playing their sport before they are eighteen: _____ percent

4. The age when children understand the idea of competition: _____
5. The number of parents who want their children to play only one sport: _____
6. Three problems with youth sports that the author describes:
   a. _____
   b. _____
   c. _____
7. The two purposes of youth sports that the author mentions:
   a. _____
   b. _____

C. Are competitive sports good or bad for children under sixteen? Give your opinion, and explain with examples and reasons.

_____

_____

_____

_____

_____

_____

_____

_____

_____

Review

Solve the crossword puzzle with vocabulary and grammar from this unit.

Across

1. a group of people who play a sport together
4. The book __ I read was interesting.
7. She won a gold __ at the Olympics last year.
8. being polite while you are playing a sport
11. The teacher __ I like the most is Dr. Kim.
12. not obey the rules in a competition
13. a group of sports teams that play together
14. The __ in the basketball game was 67–59.
15. The boots __ I bought were made in Argentina.
16. not the winner

Down

1. learning and practicing a sport
2. He scored four __ for his team.
3. a competition to find the best player or team in a sport
5. a sportsman or sportswoman
6. a person who trains athletes
8. Look at the __ to see how many points each team has.
9. a big cup for the winner of a competition
10. game

Lesson A

A. Complete the advertisement with the correct form of the words in the box.

estimate	poison	risk	survive
substance	toxic	injured	prevent

Safe at Home?

The government _____ that more than 12,000 children in this country had accidents at home last year. The _____ is highest for children under the age of five.

One of the most common household accidents is eating or drinking _____. Many of our common cleaning products contain _____ that are _____, especially to very small children. And every year, many children are _____ when they play with scissors, knives, or cigarette lighters.

Look at your house through your children's eyes, and put dangerous items in a place that kids can't reach. Keep your doctor's phone number in a place that's easy to find. Children can _____ even serious accidents if they are treated quickly.

For simple ideas on how you can _____ accidents and keep your children safe, please visit our Web site.

B. Match the sentences to the tag questions.

1. John doesn't like cats, __   a. isn't he?
2. You don't know the answer, __   b. do you?
3. He's coming to the party, __   c. are you?
4. Markus isn't in the office today, __   d. wasn't he?
5. You're not going to wear that t-shirt, __   e. doesn't she?
6. Alan got a new job, __   f. is he?
7. Salma lives in Sharjah, __   g. didn't he?
8. Nicholas was late for class, __   h. does he?

C. Add a tag question to the sentences.

1. That kind of snake is dangerous, _____?
2. They're coming back tomorrow, _____?
3. We don't have to read the whole book for class, _____?
4. You really shouldn't eat that whole cake, _____?
5. I'm right about that, _____?

Lesson B

A. Complete the chart about these dangerous jobs. Use your own knowledge and ideas.

	Reasons why someone would want to do this job	Reasons why this job is dangerous
Logger 	* You can work outdoors	* You might fall from a tree
Disaster relief worker 		
Police officer 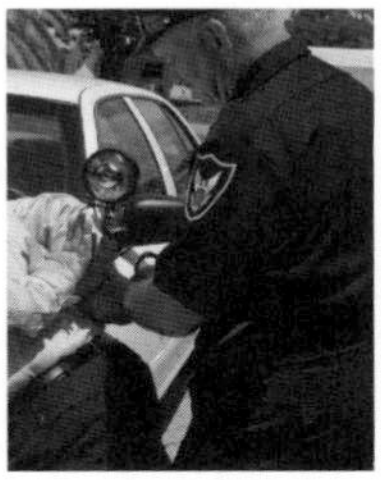		

B. Choose one of these jobs and think of a friend, family member, or classmate who would be good at it. Write about why this is a good job for this person.

_____

_____

_____

_____

_____

Lesson C

A. Read each situation and complete with a sentence from the box.

Where's the nearest pharmacy?   **Call the police!**
Where's the nearest hospital?   **Call an ambulance!**
Call the fire department!   **Where's the emergency room?**
Call a doctor!

1. You are at a concert, and a man in front of you falls on the floor. He isn't moving. You say, _"**Call a doctor!**"_

2. You work in a jewelry store. A thief runs out the door with an expensive watch. You say, "_____"

3. You have a very bad cold and you want to buy some medicine. You say, "_____ _____"

4. You're at the hospital and you need to find the place where people can see a doctor very quickly. You say, "_____"

5. You see smoke coming from a window in your school. You say, "_____ _____"

6. You are driving and you have a car accident. A woman in the other car has a bad cut and can't walk. You say, "_____"

7. Your friend has pain in his stomach and you want to take him to a clinic. You say, "_____"

B. Choose the correct word to complete each adverbial clause.

1. (As soon as/Before) I saw the smoke, I left the building.
2. Don't forget to lock the door (whenever/before) you leave the house. You have to do it every time.
3. I always take a bath (before/as soon as) I go to bed.
4. (Whenever/After) Marta called an ambulance, she tried to help the injured man.
5. (After/When) you walk in the mountains, you should watch carefully for snakes.

C. What do you do at these times? Write sentences with adverbial clauses of time.

1. as soon as you get home _____
2. before you go to bed _____
3. after you finish studying _____
4. whenever you have free time _____
5. when you want to have fun with your friends _____

Your Turn: Should Risky Sports Be Banned?

A team of mountain climbers wanted to be the first to climb a particular mountain in the winter. Then they had to be rescued by army helicopters. Nearly a hundred sailboats were participating in an ocean race when a severe storm occurred. Two sailors and one rescue worker died during the rescue mission. Adventurer Richard Branson tried to fly a balloon around the world, and crashed several times. Millions of dollars were spent to search for him and bring him home safely. We asked our readers for their opinions.

Farid: What, exactly, is a risky sport? People have died while swimming, playing soccer, or even walking, but no one says those sports are dangerous. I could get in an accident while driving to my office. You can't ban all risky sports, because people have different definitions of risky.

Jackie: Yes, they should be banned! Why should these risk takers put other people's lives in danger? And why should citizens pay all that tax money for rescue operations? Public money should not be used to help people who get into trouble with risky sports. They should be free to take any risks they want, but only if they plan ahead for rescue if they need it.

Matt: It is a personal choice to put your life at risk. We should not allow the government to put limits on our lives. If you are an adult, it should be your decision, not the government's! And if rescuers have decided to take a dangerous job, that was their choice, too. The world would be very boring if people never took risks.

Lisa: All people need a challenge. Some people really enjoy taking risks, and if high-risk sports are banned, they will feel unhappy and look for risky adventures in other areas, like business or politics, or their personal life. That would cause a lot more problems in the world.

Ramesh: They should be banned, and journalists should stop writing and talking about the things that these crazy people do. All this publicity gives a lot of bad ideas to teenagers and encourages them to try dangerous things.

A. Circle **T** for *true* or **F** for *false*.

1. According to the Web site, there have been many sports accidents recently.   T   F
2. Farid thinks people disagree about which sports are risky.   T   F
3. Jackie wants to spend more money to help people do risky sports.   T   F
4. Richard Branson had several accidents while flying in his balloon.   T   F
5. Matt thinks the government should make more rules to keep people safe.   T   F
6. Lisa thinks that risky sports are good for some people.   T   F
7. Ramesh thinks that news articles about risky sports make teenagers want to try them.   T   F
8. All of these readers want to ban risky sports.   T   F
9. Lisa thinks that banning risky sports could make people take other risks.   T   F

B. Find examples of these things on the Web page. Then add more examples of your own.

Risky sports
Sports that people think are safe
Other kinds of risks that people take

C. Write a paragraph giving your opinion. Be sure to give examples and reasons.

_____

_____

_____

_____

_____

_____

_____

_____

_____

_____

Review

Solve the crossword puzzle with vocabulary and grammar from this unit.

Across

2. I go to a movie ___ I have time.
5. He wasn't there, ___? (2 words)
7. His leg was ___ in a car accident.
9. stop from happening
10. If you see smoke in a building, you should call the fire ___.
12. containing poison
13. a place to buy medicine
15. Where's the ___ hospital?
16. You live in Bahrain, ___? (2 words)
17. guess about a number

Down

1. live through a dangerous experience
3. If you need to see a doctor quickly, go to the ___ room in the hospital.
4. It's dangerous, ___? (2 words)
6. a solid, liquid, or gas
8. They're Turkish, ___? (2 words)
11. An ___ will take you to the hospital.
13. something that will kill you if you eat it
14. possibility that something bad will happen

MYSTERIES

Lesson A

A. Complete the sentences with the correct form of the words in the box.

construct	remains	speculate	prehistoric
figure out	search	evidence	investigate

1. Scientists have found _____ that shows that the first people in our country sailed here in small wooden boats.

2. A team of scientists will _____ the kinds of tools that were used to _____ the Mayan pyramids in Mexico.

3. Scientists have _____ how people moved the big stones to build that temple. They discovered that they used boats and carried the stones on the river.

4. Tonight, rescue workers _____ for three climbers who are lost on the top of the mountain.

5. Along with the people in the old tombs, archaeologists found the _____ of horses, dogs, and other kinds of animals that they used.

6. We don't know exactly what happened to Amelia Earhart when she was flying across the Pacific. Some people _____ that she landed on a small island.

7. Archaeologists have learned a lot about _____ people by studying their tools, food, and weapons.

B. Write sentences speculating about each situation, using the verb in parentheses.

1. Sunny got 40 percent on her vocabulary test. (must) _____

   _____

2. I left a plate of cookies on the table, and now it's not there. (may) _____

   _____

3. Leo just checked his email, and now he's smiling. (might) _____

   _____

4. It's time for class, but our teacher isn't here. (could) _____

   _____

5. Nancy looks really tired today. (must) _____

   _____

C. Look at the picture. How did ancient people make this building? Write sentences speculating with *may have*, *might have*, *must have*, or *could have*.

1. _____.
2. _____.
3. _____.
4. _____.

Lesson B

A. Read the information about a mystery and answer the questions.

One of the world's strangest mysteries is a monster called the chupacabras. Some people say this animal has killed more than 2000 farm animals in Puerto Rico in recent years, such as chickens, rabbits, dogs, and even horses. The dead animals have deep holes in their necks. Often, much of their blood has been removed, but there is no blood on the ground.

Many of the attacks have occurred in an area of Puerto Rico called El Yunque, a jungle that is a national park. Much of Puerto Rico is dense jungle, which could be the home of unknown animals. Similar attacks have been reported in Costa Rica, Nicaragua, Mexico, and Brazil.

A few people say that they have seen a chupacabras. They describe an animal about one meter tall, covered in brown hair and walking on two legs. Its legs are thick and strong, but the upper part of its body is small. Other people say that the chupacabras is just a fantasy and that the animals' deaths have a natural explanation.

1. Do you think the chupacabras could be real? Explain your answer.

    _____

    _____

2. How could people prove that the chupacabras is real or not real?

    _____

    _____

3. Should scientists try to find out the truth about the chupacabras? Why, or why not?

    _____

    _____

B. Which of these mysteries would you most like to know the answer to? Circle it and explain your reasons.

> *What happened to Amelia Earhart?*
> *Why were the Nazca lines made?*
> *How did the Egyptians make the pyramids?*
> *Is there a monster in Loch Ness?*
>
> _____
> _____
> _____
> _____
> _____
> _____
> _____
> _____

Lesson C

A. Unscramble the expressions for showing surprise.

1. ttash zamniga _____

2. laryel _____

3. ryueo dikgind _____

4. blkarmaere _____

5. oww _____

B. Jessie had a lot of plans for the weekend, but she didn't do them. Write about her plans and what she did instead. Use the future in the past tense and the simple past tense.

1. Jessie was _____

2. Instead, she _____

3. _____

4. _____

5. _____

6. _____

7. _____

8. _____

C. Write about three things that you planned to do during your last vacation but didn't do. Use the future in the past tense and the simple past tense.

1. **Your plan:** _____

   What you really did: _____

2. **Your plan:** _____

   What you really did: _____

3. **Your plan:** _____

   What you really did: _____

The Mysteries of Nazca

In the desert of Peru, 300 kilometers from Lima, one of the most unusual artworks in the world has mystified people for decades. Seen from the ground, it looks like lines scratched into the earth. But from high above, these marks are huge images of birds, fish, seashells, all beautifully carved into the earth.

The Nazca lines are so difficult to see from the ground that they weren't discovered until the 1930s, when pilots spotted them while flying over the area. In all, there are about 70 different human and animal figures on the plain, along with 900 triangles, circles, and lines.

Researchers have figured out that the lines are at least 1500 years old, but their purpose is still a mystery.

In the 1940s, an American explorer named Paul Kosok suggested that the drawings were a chronicle of the movement of the stars and planets. He called Nazca "the largest astronomy book in the world." Later, an astronomer tested his theory with a computer, but he couldn't find any relation between the lines and movements in space.

Another explanation is that the lines may have been made for religious reasons. British researcher Tony Morrison investigated the customs of people in the Andes Mountains and learned that they sometimes pray by the side of the road. It's possible that in the past, the lines of Nazca were created for a similar purpose. The largest pictures may have been the sites for special ceremonies. But the local people have never constructed anything this big.

Recently, two other scientists, David Johnson and Steve Mabee, have speculated that the lines could have been related to water. Nazca is one of the driest places in the world and receives only 2 cm of rain every year. While Johnson was searching for ancient water sources in the area, he noticed that some waterways built by ancient people were connected with the lines. Johnson believes that the Nazca lines are a giant map of the underground water in the area. Other scientists are now searching for evidence to prove this.

A. Read the article and complete the chart.

Person	Theory	Evidence for or against this theory
Paul Kosok	*The Nazca lines are* _____ _____	
Tony Morrison		
David Johnson Steve Mabee		

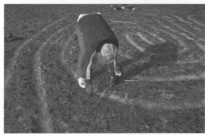

B. Look at the underlined words in the reading and try to guess their meaning without using your dictionary.

1. *Spotted* probably means ___.
    a. saw   b. crashed into   c. made

2. *Tricky* probably means ___.
    a. interesting   b. easy   c. difficult

3. A *chronicle* probably means ___.
    a. a speculation   b. a history   c. a theory

4. *Waterway* probably means ___.
    a. something to drink   b. a kind of pot   c. a narrow place that carries water

C. Is it important to find the answers to mysteries like this? Why, or why not?

_____
_____
_____
_____
_____
_____

Review

Solve the crossword puzzle with vocabulary and grammar from this unit.

Across

1. look for
4. Hani isn't in class today. He __ be sick.
8. You say this when you are surprised.
9. "I saw a chupacabras." "__?"
12. guess about something
14. "You saw a sea monster?" "You're __!"
15. Some people still want to __ what happened to Amelia Earhart.
16. Scientists are trying to __ out how people moved the stones in the pyramids.

Down

2. build
3. The Nazca lines __ be a giant map.
5. Scientists __ soon know the answer.
6. before written history
7. "The Pyramids in Egypt are more than 6000 years old." "That's __!"
8. We __ do our homework last night, but we watched a movie instead. (3 words)
9. the parts of something that are left after the rest of it is gone
10. I __ be an engineer when I grew up. (3 words)
11. very surprising
13. clues that show something is true

Lesson A

A. Complete the advertisement with words from the box.

semester	campus	course	enroll	tuition
scholarships	major	apply	required	deadline

Living English, every day!

Living English is an exciting four-month _____ in the United States and Canada. Students live on the _____ of a local university and take special _____ in North American history, literature, and culture, along with English classes in small groups. We have programs in Seattle, Miami, or Toronto; one of them is perfect for you!

You don't need to be an English _____ to be a part of Living English; students in any field can _____ in this program and experience life in North America, but intermediate level English is _____. The _____ for this program is $3000, but we have _____ available to help you pay for the cost.

The _____ is March 1st, so be sure to _____ soon. For more information, please visit our Web site.

B. Write answers to your friend. Use *should (not) have*, *could have*, or *would have* and the verb in parentheses.

1. **Your friend:** I watched movies until 2:00 a.m. last night. Now I'm really tired.
   You: (go to bed) _____.

2. **Your friend:** I didn't eat lunch because I left my wallet at home.
   You: (lend) _____.

3. **Your friend:** I'm sorry you had to wait for me for an hour. My car broke down.
   You: (call) _____.

4. **Your friend:** I'm really upset. I've gained 10 kilos this year!
   You: (eat) _____.

5. **Your friend:** Our teacher looks angry with me. I wonder why?
   You: (do) _____.

6. **Your friend:** I spent 10 hours cleaning my apartment because my parents are coming to visit.
   You: (call) _____.

C. Write sentences about these things with *should (not) have*, *could have*, or *would have*.

1. A mistake you made _____

2. Something you didn't try _____

3. Something you wish you had done _____

Lesson B

A. Fill in the name of the learning style.

| Auditory   Visual   Kinesthetic   Reading/writing |

1. _____ learners like to use their eyes to take in information.
2. _____ learners use printed words to get new information.
3. _____ learners take in information by using their bodies.
4. _____ learners like to get new information by hearing it.

B. Read what these people say about their experiences. What is each person's learning style?

1. Alicia says: "I tried to learn Chinese once, but I didn't get very far. The lessons just weren't right for me. The teacher was really nice—she was from Beijing—and she was going to teach me conversation. She said that writing Chinese is difficult, so it's better to just learn speaking. Well, we practiced all kinds of sentences, but I could never remember them. I forgot them as soon as she said them. To remember things, I really need to see them written down. Next time, I want to take a class that uses a textbook."

   Alicia is a/an _____ learner.

2. Brandon says: "I had so many problems in school when I was younger! It was hard for me to sit at a desk all day and just listen and write. I was bored all the time, so I caused a lot of trouble for the teachers. I'm really glad that I went to a technical high school. I studied computer repair, and I finally had some interesting classes where I could use my hands to do something. Now I have a great job in an electronics store, because I learned how to do something useful."

   Brandon is a/an_____ learner.

C. Which learning style are these activities good for? Write each activity in the correct box.

looking at paintings in a museum   doing a science experiment
practicing a dance   using a map of Africa
watching a video about nature   using books from the library
attending a lecture   listening to an author reading his poems
making a cake   finding new words in the dictionary
looking for information on a Web site

Auditory	Visual
Reading/Writing	**Kinesthetic**

Lesson C

A. Match the name of the major with the things students learn about.

1. economics ___
2. education ___
3. agriculture ___
4. law ___
5. business ___
6. engineering ___
7. psychology ___
8. chemistry___
9. social work___
10. geology ___

a. how the human mind works
b. raising food, plants, and animals
c. designing machines, roads, bridges, etc.
d. how people learn
e. Earth and its rocks and minerals
f. how different substances react together
g. why companies succeed or fail
h. the money system in a country
i. helping people with family or social problems
j. the legal system in a country

B. Underline the noun clauses in these sentences.

1. What you told me was really interesting.
2. I don't remember where I bought that book.
3. In that class, students learn about how the earth and its rocks were formed.
4. Sayeed can tell you how to get to the new mall.
5. I can really understand why she felt so nervous.
6. My friends told me what I should do.

C. Anita and Janie are talking about Janie's new roommate. Write Janie's answers using the words in parentheses and noun clauses.

1. **Anita:** Where did you first meet her?
   Janie: (not remember) _I don't remember where I first met her._
2. **Anita:** Why is she moving house?
   Janie: (have no idea) _____
3. **Anita:** What kind of a job does she have?
   Janie: (not sure) _____
4. **Anita:** Who are her friends?
   Janie: (not know) _____
5. **Anita:** When can I meet her?
   Janie: (not know) _____

Students Return from Adventure Abroad

Four students from National University have recently returned from Africa, where they participated in development projects with local residents in rural areas. For 10 weeks, these young men worked in Zimbabwe and Botswana as members of a program called Raleigh International.

Raleigh International, founded by the Prince of Wales in 1984, gives young people a chance to do volunteer work while experiencing other countries and **their** cultures. The program, named after the explorer Sir Walter Raleigh, encourages young people to help others and work in difficult settings. More than 30,000 students from a variety of cultures and backgrounds have volunteered in a total of 40 countries.

James Hendon, 20, a business major, traveled to Zimbabwe to work with a group in the Mavuradonha Wilderness Area. Their first project was helping farmers build electric fences to keep elephants from destroying **their** crops. When elephants entered the village one night, the students joined with farmers to drive **them** away and preserve the fields. Hendon's group also constructed small cottages for tourists to stay in, built in the local style.

Saeed Mohammed, also 20 and an engineering major, joined another group in Zimbabwe. His group carried out a survey of health problems in several villages and taught children about good health habits. Saeed said the kids were so curious about the Raleigh International students that after the health lessons, they asked **them** questions about "everything else under the sun."

Saeed's group also worked to build foot trails through the forest. While they were out working in the bush, a fire broke out, destroying eight kilometers of forest. The students fought to bring the fire under control, sleeping only 45 minutes during the two days that it raged.

In Botswana, two 19-year-old students, Lewis Young and David Min, helped to build a clinic and a meeting hall in a small village. Though they didn't face angry elephants, they said the building work was much harder than they expected. "It was a great learning experience," Young said.

After all the hard work, the four students found time for fun. They took boat trips, learned African poems, and traveled together for a week after **their** program ended.

A. Find the information in the article.

1. two countries where the students did volunteer work _____, _____

2. the name of the volunteer program _____

3. the year the program started _____

4. the number of people who have volunteered with the program since it began _____

5. five projects that the students worked on _____, _____, _____, _____, _____

6. two dangerous situations that the students faced _____, _____

7. three things that the students did to relax _____, _____, _____

B. Look back at the reading and find what each of the pronouns in **bold** refers to.

1. **their** (par. 2)
   a. Wales　　　b. young people　　　c. countries　　　d. settings

2. **their** (par. 3)
   a. group　　　b. farmers　　　c. fences　　　d. elephants

3. **them** (par. 3)
   a. crops　　　b. students　　　c. elephants　　　d. farmers

4. **them** (par. 4)
   a. kids　　　b. health　　　c. lessons　　　d. students

5. **their** (par. 7)
   a. students　　　b. boats　　　c. poems　　　d. programs

C. Write about a difficult experience that you learned something from.

_____

_____

_____

_____

_____

_____

_____

_____

_____

Review

Solve the crossword puzzle with vocabulary and grammar from this unit.

Across

1. an area of land with university buildings
3. a series of lessons in one subject
5. the study of legal systems
6. I _____ said hello, but I didn't see you. (2 words)
7. the study of the human mind
8. the study of the earth and its rocks
11. something that you must have
13. the main subject you are studying
17. I _____ eaten so much ice cream. It was a bad idea. (2 words)

Down

1. I _____ studied in Canada. It was possible. (2 words)
2. half of a school year
4. Andy got a __. He got $5000 to pay for college because he's an excellent student.
9. the study of how food is grown in farms
10. the study of designing and making buildings or machines
12. the study of money
14. money you pay for education
15. join a class or school
16. I liked __ you said.

Lesson A

A. Complete the sentences with the correct form of the words in the box.

exploration	satellite	orbit	universe	manned
unmanned	planet	discover	colonize	mission

1. Some people think that we should send people to _____ Mars, because Earth has become too polluted to live on.

2. The first _____ space flight was in 1961. It was made by a Russian named Yuri Gagarin.

3. Before Gagarin flew in space, there were other _____ flights that carried dogs.

4. Earth and the other planets _____ around the sun.

5. The _____ of space has given us valuable information for scientists and helped to develop many important products that we use every day.

6. Venus and Mars are the _____ closest to us.

7. The last _____ to the moon was in 1975.

8. Today, we use_____ for communication, observing the weather, and many other purposes.

9. Some people think that we will soon _____ living things on other planets.

10. The _____ contains many stars and planets that we don't know about now.

Mercury
Venus
Earth
Mars
Jupiter
Saturn
Uranus
Neptune

B. Will people live on other planets in the future? Write your predictions with *will* or *going to*.

1. _____
2. _____
3. _____
4. _____

C. Circle the verb forms that make correct sentences about the future. More than one answer may be correct, with different meanings.

1. The weather forecast said it _____ tomorrow.
   a. will snow   b. is going to snow   c. snows   d. is snowing

2. "We don't have any more coffee.""I _____ to the store and get some."
   a. 'll go   b. am going to go   c. go   d. am going

3. The test _____ at 10:00 a.m.
   a. will start   b. is going to start   c. starts   d. is starting

4. In the year 2020, people _____ vacations in space.
   a. will take   b. are going to take   c. take   d. are taking

Lesson B

A. The government of your country has decided to send one "citizen astronaut" to spend a month at the International Space Station. There are three candidates. Read the information and make notes about each candidate.

Lydia is a science teacher at a high school. She has always been interested in the universe, and she loves teaching students about space. She is 43 years old and has five children. Her health is good, but she can't see very well without her glasses. Reason for wanting to travel in space: "I can share my experiences with my students and with all the other young people in our country."

Positive:	Negative:

Ryan is 28 years old. He is a professional athlete and a member of the national soccer team, which did very well in the last World Cup championship. He is engaged and will marry his girlfriend next year. His health is excellent, even though he smokes cigarettes. Reason for wanting to travel in space: "All my life I have loved adventure, and space is the biggest adventure of all."

Positive:	Negative:

Ahmed is a doctor at a free clinic for poor people. Many people admire his work. He is 51 years old, and his health is fair. He got very sick last year from overworking, but he feels better now. He is married, and his two children are adults. Reason for wanting to travel in space: "Exploring the universe gives us hope. I want to bring that hope to everyone on Earth."

Positive:	Negative:

B. Who should be the citizen astronaut? Write about your opinion and explain your reasons.

_____

_____

_____

_____

C. Write these compound nouns correctly (one word, two words, or hyphenated). Then say them out loud.

1. space + craft _____
2. follow + up _____
3. back + pack _____
4. space + station _____
5. life + saver _____
6. check + in _____
7. hard + ware _____
8. space + walk _____
9. bed + room _____
10. fruit + juice _____

Lesson C

A. Match the parts of these time expressions.

1. in a little ___   a. these days
2. someday ___   b. soon
3. one ___   c. years
4. one of ___   d. while
5. in 10 ___   e. later
6. sooner or ___   f. day

B. Write sentences about the future using *may*, *might*, or *could*.

people/start colonies on the moon

_____

new medicines/cure cancer

_____

astronauts/find living things on other planets

_____

scientists/live permanently in space

_____

new planets/be found far away in the universe

_____

C. Complete the sentences about the future with *be able to*, *have to*, or *need to* and the verb in parentheses.

1. My plane leaves at 6:00 a.m. I (go) **I will have to go**_____ to the airport very early.
2. I can play a few songs on my guitar now. After I take guitar lessons, I (play) _____ a lot of songs.
3. If people take vacations in space, they (see) _____ beautiful views of Earth.
4. My parents' anniversary is on Friday. I (buy) _____ them a present before then.
5. There isn't any air on the moon. Space colonists (bring) _____ air with them from Earth.
6. I just bought a new camera. I (take) _____ much better pictures with it.

D. What do you think the world will be like a hundred years from now? Complete the sentences with your ideas.

1. _____ might _____.
2. _____ may _____.
3. _____ could _____.

First in Space

The first person to travel in space was Yuri Gagarin. He was born in a small village in Russia (in the Soviet Union) on September 3, 1934. His parents were farmers. He went to work in a steel factory while he was still very young, but he was later chosen to go to a technical high school to study engineering. There, he joined a flying club, and learned how to fly small airplanes. At least he knew what he wanted to do with his life.

After he finished his education, he trained to become a military pilot, and he was sent to an air base in the Arctic. The bad weather there made flying extremely difficult, and Gagarin became a highly skilled flyer. In 1960 he was appointed to be in the first group of Soviet astronauts, or *cosmonauts*. Gagarin excelled in this training, because he was very intelligent and also very short. The first spacecraft were very small inside, and Gagarin was only 157 cm (62 inches) tall.

On April 12, 1961, Gagarin became the first person to fly in space in his spacecraft, Vostok 1. He orbited Earth for 1 hour and 48 minutes. The spacecraft was flown by computers, so during his time in space, he ate and drank, and looked down at our planet, for the first time in history. "The Earth is blue," he said, over the radio. "How wonderful. It is amazing." He also sang a patriotic song about Russia. Although he experienced problems with his spacecraft, he landed safely in a farm field.

After his historic flight, Gagarin was a celebrity. He traveled in Italy, Canada, Germany, and Japan and gave lectures about his experience. He desperately wanted to travel in space again, but as a national hero, he was not allowed by the government to risk his life. Instead, he trained other astronauts and pilots. He also worked on a design for a reusable spacecraft, but it was never built. Gagarin died in a flying accident on March 27, 1968. The cause of the accident is still not known.

A. Circle **T** for *true* or **F** for *false* or **NI** for *no information* (if the answer is not in the reading).

1.   The first person in space was American.   T   F   NI
2.   Yuri Gagarin learned to fly airplanes as a student.   T   F   NI
3.   Astronauts today are usually very tall.   T   F   NI
4.   Gagarin stayed in space for more than one day.   T   F   NI
5.   Vostok 1 used computers to fly.   T   F   NI
6.   Gagarin visited other countries to talk about being an astronaut.   T   F   NI
7.   Gagarin flew in space several times.   T   F   NI
8.   Gagarin died after an accident in a spacecraft.   T   F   NI

B. Write numbers to put the sentences in chronological order.

___ Gagarin became a military pilot.

___ Gagarin worked in a factory.

___ Gagarin became extremely famous.

___ Gagarin learned to fly.

___ Gagarin was picked to be an astronaut.

___ Gagarin invented a new kind of spacecraft.

___ Vostok 1 was the first manned mission in space.

C. Do you think governments should spend money for space exploration? Give your opinion, and explain your reasons.

_____

_____

_____

_____

_____

_____

_____

_____

Review

Solve the crossword puzzle with vocabulary and grammar from this unit.

Across

3. The phone is ringing. I __ answer it.
6. One of __, I'm going to clean out all the closets in my house. (2 words)
8. go in a circle around something
11. all of space, the planets, and the stars
12. Jason __ to look for another job. I'm not sure if he will do it.
14. send people to live in a new place
15. __ day, we will travel to distant stars.
16. looking for new things
18. The concert tomorrow __ at eight o'clock.

Down

1. In a little __, I'm going to take a computer class.
2. In the future, people __ live to be 150 years old. It's possible.
4. Sooner or __, people will walk on the moon again.
5. Someday __, we will find a cure for cancer.
7. Today we use __ for the weather and communication.
9. I can't swim now. After I take lessons, I will __ swim. (3 words)
10. We (go) __ to Egypt on our vacation next month. (2 words)
13. Earth, Mars, or Jupiter
17. __ 10 years, I will be an old woman.

VOCABULARY INDEX